Other books in the series:
The Crazy World of Birdwatching (Peter Rigby)
The Crazy World of Cats (Bill Stott)
The Crazy World of Cricket (Bill Stott)
The Crazy World of Gardening (Bill Stott)
The Crazy World of Golf (Mike Scott)
The Crazy World of the Handyman (Roland Fiddy)
The Crazy World of Hospitals (Bill Stott)
The Crazy World of Jogging (David Pye)
The Crazy World of Love (Roland Fiddy)
The Crazy World of Marriage (Bill Stott)
The Crazy World of Music (Bill Stott)
The Crazy World of Photography (Bill Stott)
The Crazy World of Rugby (Bill Stott)
The Crazy World of Sailing (Peter Rigby)
The Crazy World of the School (Bill Stott)
The Crazy World of Sex (David Pye)
The Crazy World of Skiing (Craig Peterson & Jerry Emerson)
The Crazy World of Tennis (Peter Rigby)

Published in Great Britain in 1991 by
**Exley Publications Ltd, 16 Chalk Hill,**
**Watford, Herts WD1 4BN, United Kingdom.**

**ISBN 1-85015-221-7**

Printed and bound in Spain

# the CRAZY world of the ROYALS

### Cartoons by
### Barry Knowles

**≡EXLEY**

"*Would your majesty please throw the salt...?*"

*"... and give us this day relief from the usual seventeen course embassy banquet..."*

"I keep imagining I'm one of my own loyal subjects..."

*"I don't carry cash – will you settle for a couple of medals…?"*

"It's an idea of an ancestor of mine – I'm commanding the oil slick to go back..."

*"I'm a computer programmer, madam – what's your line...?"*

"The power behind the throne has blown a fuse..."

"*Your mother's putting on a spot of weight…*"

"*Wait till the lights go down and we'll sneak out through the emergency exit...*"

"*The economy must be in a worse state than I thought...*"

*"Is it you or mother who's descended from King Kong?"*

*"Knock me off the following, old thing: opening of parliament, three state visits, a meeting of industrialists, a hospital extension, new hovercraft terminal, a tree planting, seven plaque unveilings and a few gags for a radio phone-in..."*

PHOTOS

WITH SMILE
£2

WITH WINK
£5·00

SCRATCHING
NOSE
£10·00

"I popped into the nursery today and bought this for Charles..."

"That's where I left my umbrella – in the Galapagos Islands…"

"*I've been signed off royal walkabouts and handshakes for a month...*"

"*Did you hear the one about the English king, the Scottish king and the Irish king...?*"

*"Summon your scriptwriters..."*

HIS    HEIRS

Barry Knowles

"I hadn't realized we were that hard up..."

"... and twenty Queen size tipped..."

*"She's just made her first royal proclamation…"*

*"Come on! Royal walkabouts!"*

"He's just read your bill from the betting office..."

*"Gosh! One ought to have been reviewing the troops three hours ago..."*

*"One's damned embarrassed by winning the raffle at one's own garden party…"*

BanyKnowles

"I've written a daring exposé of life among the household servants..."

"I see the Black Prince is staying with us again..."

"*Believe me, it's a relief to get away from vintage champagne, five star brandy and fine old crusted port...*"

"I recognize that one – I was a Mickey Mouse club
member myself..."

"... and this is my first wife..."

"Boys! That is <u>not</u> the way we conduct royal walkabouts..."

*"Why do we hire a nanny, Charles? Let's follow the example of your ancestors and lock them up in the tower..."*

*"Call out the emergency services.... We've just sunk the royal yacht..."*

*"Missus, you've got one hell of a wrong number..."*

*"Look – the first royal wee..."*

*"'Ere gov, aren't you supposed to be up on the balcony...?"*

*"Mum, they've cancelled Tom and Jerry for your rotten old Queen's speech..."*

*"You get a small income for every polo injury or a lump sum
in case of abdication..."*

"*What happened to all the red areas...?*"

"What do you mean – do we have any means of identification...?"

*"Remind me to fire the poet laureate…"*

*"Yes, it's very realistic – your great, great grandfather poured a vat of molten lead over a double glazing salesman…"*

"That's agreed then — we demand index-linked pensions after abdication, free travel and double-time for launching ships..."

*"I'll be glad when cook gets back..."*

*"Ignore him – he's on our Awards Scheme..."*

*"It gives me great pleasure to declare this six-pack of beer well and truly open..."*

"*Poor Fanshaw! He's never got the hang of walking out of doors backwards…*"

"It's stopped reigning..."

"Is there something I haven't been told...?"

NATIONAL ANTHEM
STATEMENT OF
ROYALTIES

BarryKnowles

*"Sorry about the old newspapers sir – the moths have got at the red carpet..."*

"You're smiling and waving in your sleep again..."

"*Must we send Christmas cards to every one of the common multitude?*"

# Books from the "Crazy World" series:

**The Crazy World of Birdwatching.** £3.99. By Peter Rigby. Over seventy cartoons on the strange antics of the twitcher brigade. One of our most popular pastimes, this will be a natural gift for any birdwatcher.

**The Crazy World of Cats.** £3.99. By Bill Stott. Fat cats, alley cats, lazy cats, sneaky cats – from the common moggie to the pedigree Persian – you'll find them all in this witty collection. If you've ever wondered what your cat was really up to, this is for you.

**The Crazy World of Cricket.** £3.99. By Bill Stott. This must be Bill Stott's silliest cartoon collection. It makes an affectionate present for any cricketer who can laugh at himself.

**The Crazy World of Gardening.** £3.99. By Bill Stott. The perfect present for anyone who has ever wrestled with a lawnmower that won't start, over-watered a pot plant or been assaulted by a rose bush from behind.

**The Crazy World of Golf.** £3.99. By Mike Scott. Over seventy hilarious cartoons show the fanatic golfer in his (or her) every absurdity. What really goes on out on the course, and the golfer's life when not playing are chronicled in loving detail.

**The Crazy World of the Handyman.** £3.99. By Roland Fiddy. This book is a must for anyone who has ever hung *one* length of wallpaper upside down or drilled through an electric cable. A gift for anyone who has ever tried to "do it yourself" and failed!

**The Crazy World of Hospitals.** £3.99. By Bill Stott. Hilarious cartoons about life in a hospital. A perfect present for a doctor or a nurse – or a patient who needs a bit of fun.

**The Crazy World of Love.** £3.99. By Roland Fiddy. This funny yet tender collection covers every aspect of love from its first joys to its dying embers. An ideal gift for lovers of all ages to share with each other.

**The Crazy World of Marriage.** £3.99. By Bill Stott. The battle of the sexes in close-up from the altar to the grave, in public and in private, in and out of bed. See your friends, your enemies (and possibly yourselves?) as never before!

**The Crazy World of Music.** £3.99. By Bill Stott. This upbeat collection will delight music-lovers of all ages. From Beethoven to Wagner and from star conductor to the humblest orchestra member, no-one escapes Bill Stott's penetrating pen.

**The Crazy World of the Office.** £3.99. By Bill Stott. Laugh your way through the office jungle with Bill Stott as he observes the idiosyncrasies of bosses, the deviousness of underlings and the goings-on at the Christmas party.... A must for anyone who has ever worked in an office!

**The Crazy World of Photography.** £3.99. By Bill Stott. Everyone who owns a camera, be it a Box Brownie or the latest Pentax, will find something to laugh at in this superb collection. The absurdities of the camera freak will delight your whole family.

**The Crazy World of Rugby.** £3.99. By Bill Stott. From schoolboy to top international player, no-one who plays or watches rugby will escape Bill Stott's merciless exposé of their habits and absurdities. Over seventy hilarious cartoons – a must for addicts.

**The Crazy World of Sailing.** £3.99. By Peter Rigby. The perfect present for anyone who has ever messed about in boats, gone pea-green in a storm or been stuck in the doldrums.

**The Crazy World of the School.** £3.99. By Bill Stott. A brilliant and hilarious reminder of those chalk-throwing days. Wince at Bill Stott's wickedly funny new collection of crazy school capers.

**The Crazy World of Sex.** £3.99. By David Pye. A light-hearted look at the absurdities and weaker moments of human passion – the turn-ons and the turn-offs. Very funny and in (reasonably) good taste.

**The Crazy World of Skiing.** £3.99. By Craig Peterson and Jerry Emerson. Covering almost every possible (and impossible) experience on the slopes, this is an ideal present for anyone who has ever strapped on skis – and instantly fallen over.

These books make super presents. Order them from your local bookseller or from Exley Publications Ltd, Dept BP, 16 Chalk Hill, Watford, Herts WD1 4BN. (Please send £1.50 for one book or £2.25 for two or more to cover postage and packing.)